NOTE-FOR-NOTE TRANSCRIPTIONS

100 GREAT
KEYBOARD
INTROS

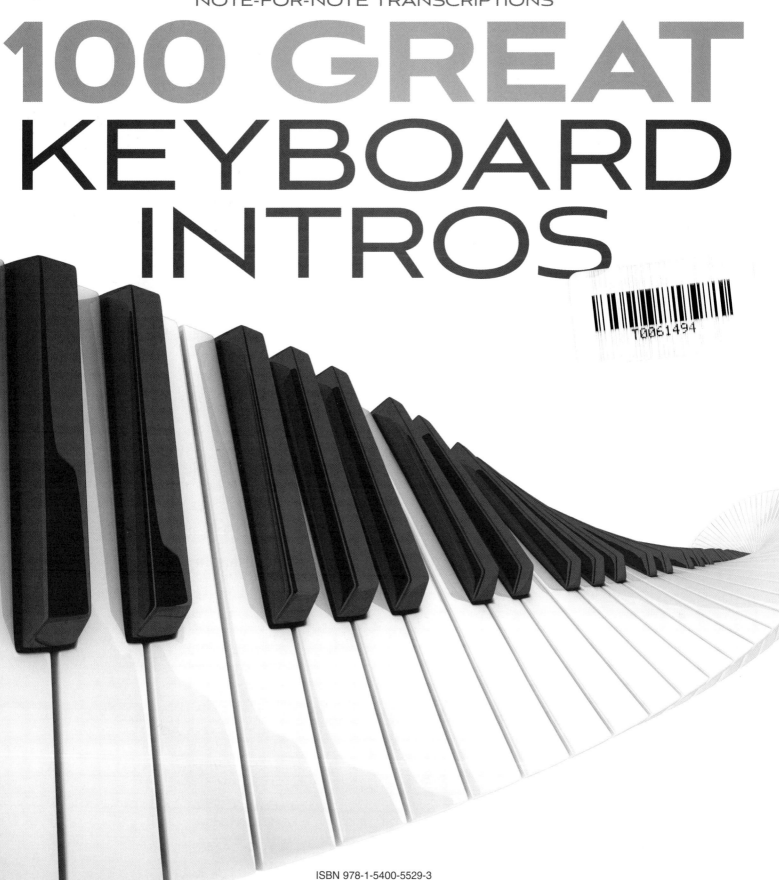

ISBN 978-1-5400-5529-3

HAL•LEONARD®

Visit Hal Leonard Online at
www.halleonard.com

Contact us:
Hal Leonard
7777 West Bluemound Road
Milwaukee, WI 53213
Email: info@halleonard.com

In Europe, contact:
Hal Leonard Europe Limited
42 Wigmore Street
Marylebone, London, W1U 2RN
Email: info@halleonardeurope.com

In Australia, contact:
Hal Leonard Australia Pty. Ltd.
4 Lentara Court
Cheltenham, Victoria, 3192 Australia
Email: info@halleonard.com.au

CONTENTS

Against All Odds
(Take a Look at Me Now)

Words and Music by Phil Collins

All of Me

Words and Music by John Stephens and Toby Gad

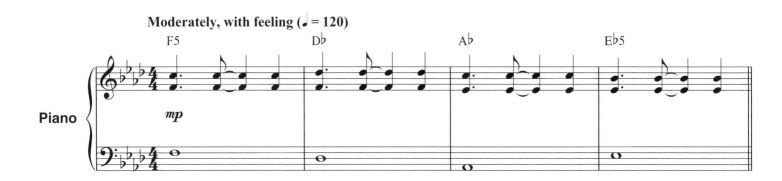

Alone

Words and Music by Billy Steinberg and Tom Kelly

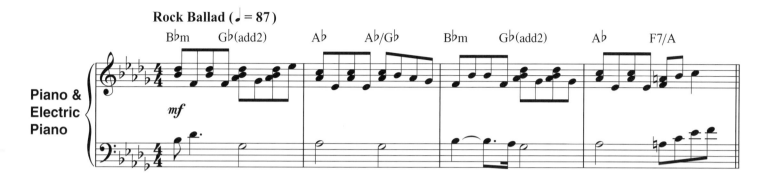

And So It Goes

Words and Music by Billy Joel

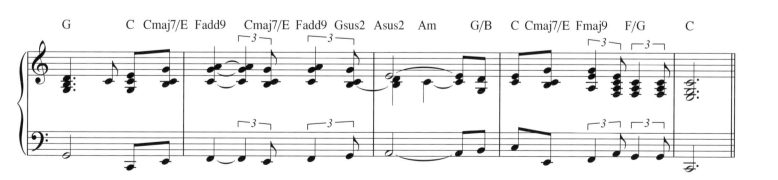

Axel F
Theme from the Paramount Motion Picture BEVERLY HILLS COP
By Harold Faltermeyer

Babe
Words and Music by Dennis DeYoung

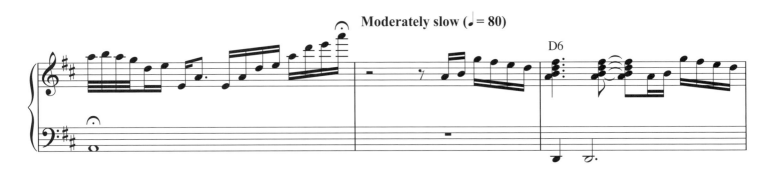

Bennie and the Jets

Words and Music by Elton John and Bernie Taupin

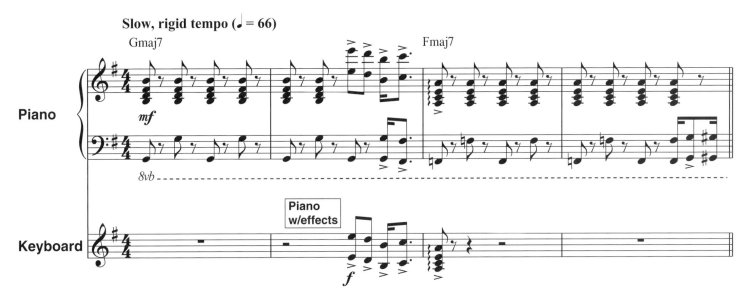

Bless the Broken Road

Words and Music by Marcus Hummon,
Bobby Boyd and Jeff Hanna

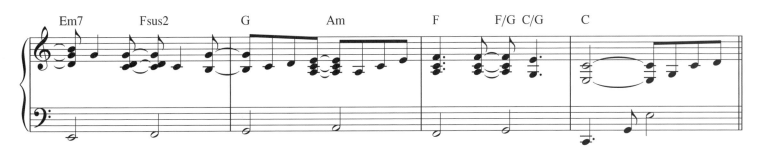

Bloody Well Right

Words and Music by Rick Davies
and Roger Hodgson

Blueberry Hill

Words and Music by Al Lewis, Larry Stock
and Vincent Rose

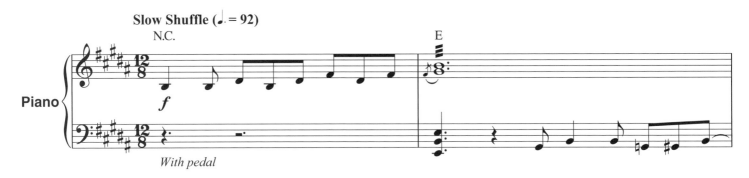

Bridge Over Troubled Water

Words and Music by Paul Simon

Brick

Words and Music by Ben Folds and Darren Jessee

Not too fast (♩ = 100)

Clocks

Words and Music by Guy Berryman, Jon Buckland,
Will Champion and Chris Martin

Moderately (♩ = 130)

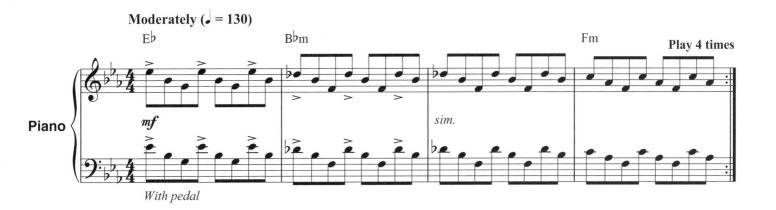

(They Long to Be)
Close to You

Lyric by Hal David
Music by Burt Bacharach

Moderate Ballad (♩ = 89)

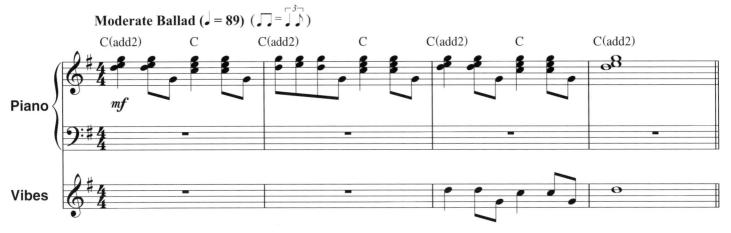

Cold as Ice

Words and Music by Mick Jones and Lou Gramm

Moderate Rock (♩ = 130)

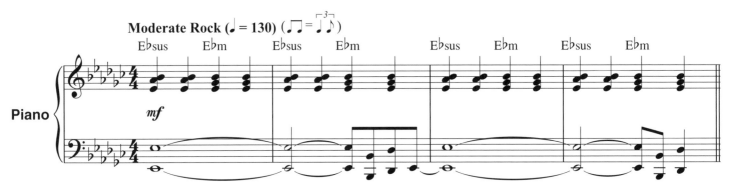

Come Sail Away

Words and Music by Dennis DeYoung

Moderately slow, with feeling (♩ = 70)

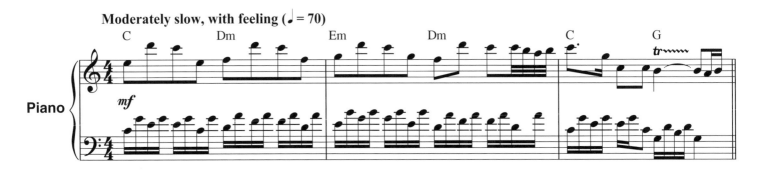

Crazy

Words and Music by Willie Nelson

Piano, organ, guitar and bass arranged for piano.

Deacon Blues

Words and Music by Walter Becker and Donald Fagen

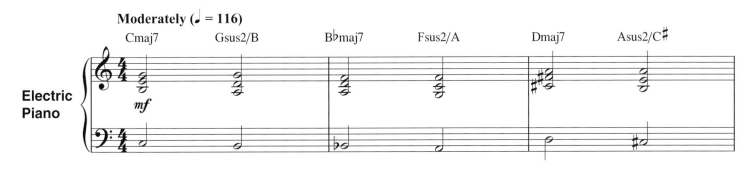

Don't Know Much

Words and Music by Barry Mann,
Cynthia Weil and Tom Snow

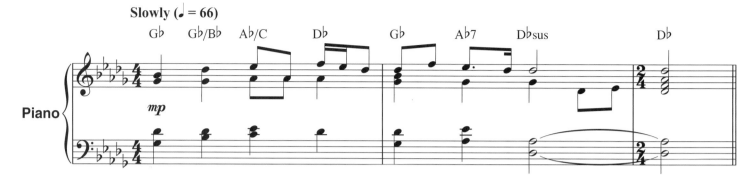

Don't Let the Sun Go Down on Me

Words and Music by Elton John and Bernie Taupin

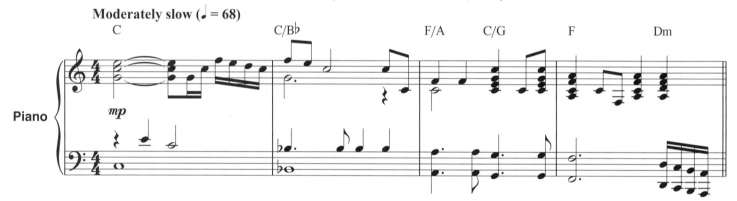

Down

Words and Music by Samantha Gongol and Jeremy Lloyd

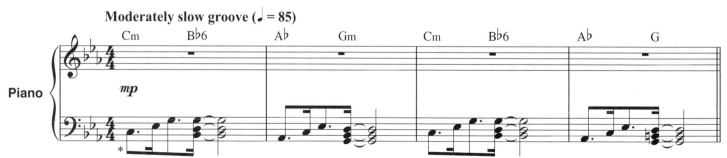

* *Play the first L.H. note of each measure staccato.*

Dream On

Words and Music by Steven Tyler

Drops of Jupiter
(Tell Me)

Words and Music by Pat Monahan, Jimmy Stafford, Robert Hotchkiss,
Charles Colin and Scott Underwood

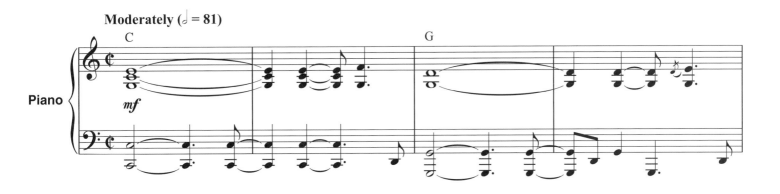

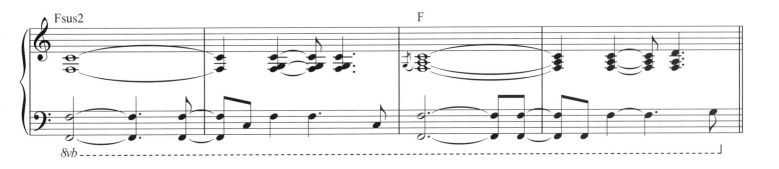

Easy
Words and Music by Lionel Richie

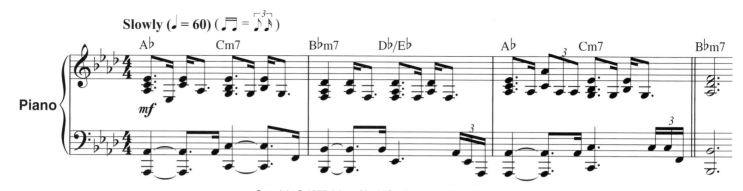

Endless Love
Words and Music by Lionel Richie

Faithfully
Words and Music by Jonathan Cain

Final Countdown

Words and Music by Joey Tempest

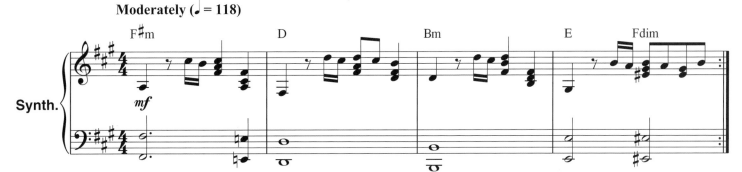

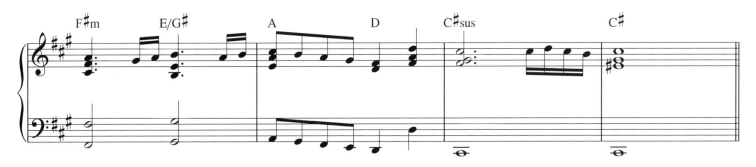

Glory of Love

Theme from KARATE KID PART II

Words and Music by David Foster, Peter Cetera and Diane Nini

Piano and electric piano arranged for piano.

The Greatest Love of All

Words by Linda Creed
Music by Michael Masser

Moderately slow (♩ = 72)

Hard Habit to Break

Words and Music by Stephen Kipner and John Lewis Parker

Moderately slow (♩ = 81)

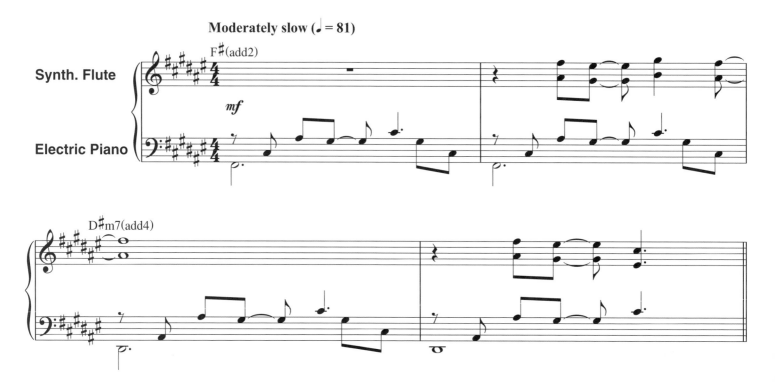

Hard To Say I'm Sorry

Words and Music by Peter Cetera and David Foster

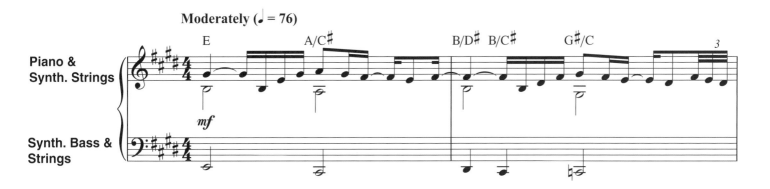

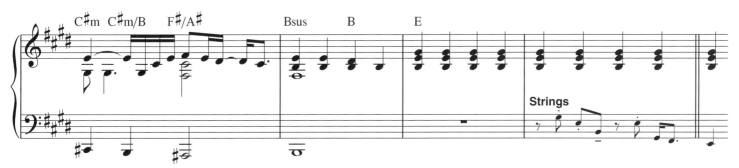

Hold the Line

Words and Music by David Paich

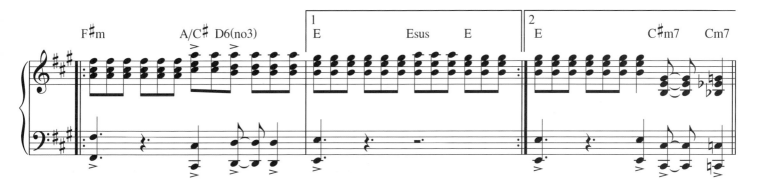

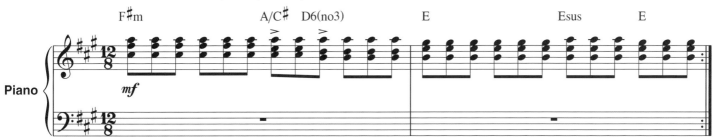

Honky Cat

Words and Music by Elton John and Bernie Taupin

I Am the Walrus

Words and Music by John Lennon and Paul McCartney

Hero

Words and Music by Mariah Carey and Walter Afanasieff

I Don't Know

Words and Music by Paul McCartney

(Everything I Do)
I Do It for You

from the Motion Picture ROBIN HOOD: PRINCE OF THIEVES

Words and Music by Bryan Adams, R.J. Lange and Michael Kamen

I Guess That's Why
They Call It the Blues

Words and Music by Elton John, Bernie Taupin and Davey Johnstone

I Feel the Earth Move
Words and Music by Carole King

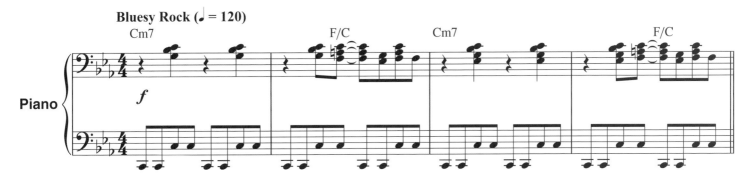

I Write the Songs
Words and Music by Bruce Johnston

I'll Be There
Words and Music by Berry Gordy Jr., Hal Davis,
Willie Hutch and Bob West

If I Ain't Got You

Words and Music by Alicia Keys

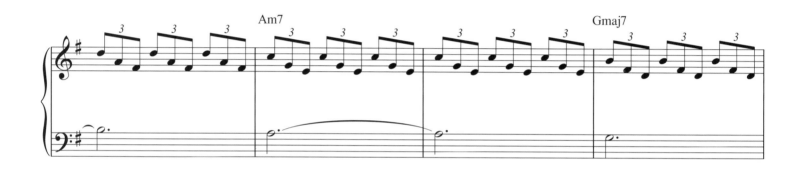

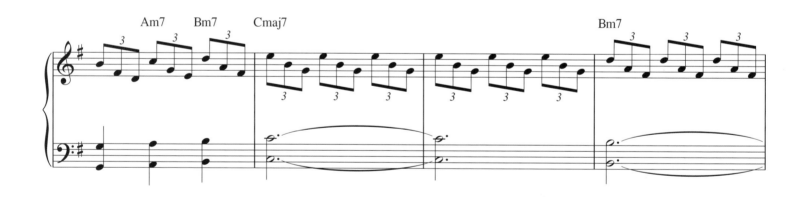

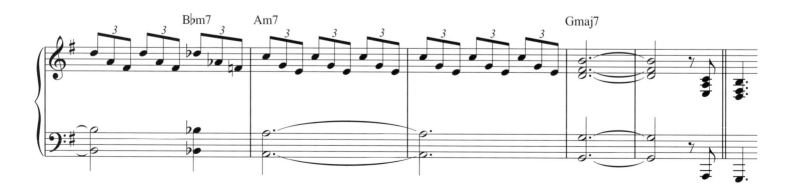

I'll Never Love Again
from A STAR IS BORN

Words and Music by Stefani Germanotta, Aaron Raitiere,
Hillary Lindsey and Natalie Hemby

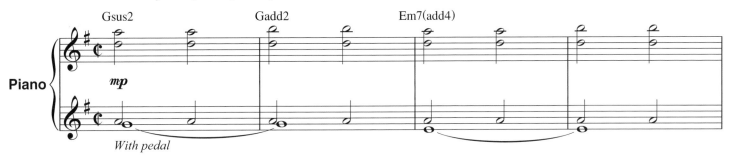

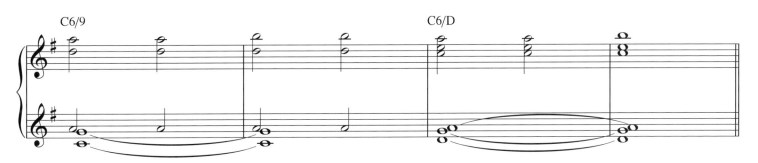

It's Too Late

Words and Music by Carole King and Toni Stern

Jump

Words and Music by Edward Van Halen, Alex Van Halen and David Lee Roth

Just the Two of Us

Words and Music by Ralph MacDonald, William Salter and Bill Withers

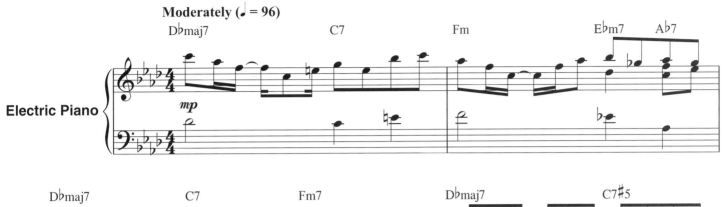

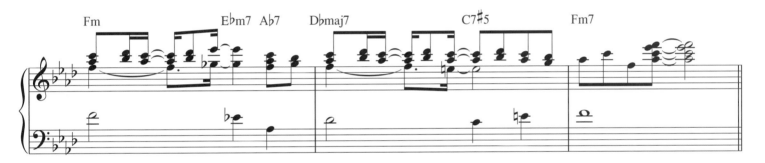

Imagine

Words and Music by John Lennon

Just Once

Words by Cynthia Weil
Music by Barry Mann

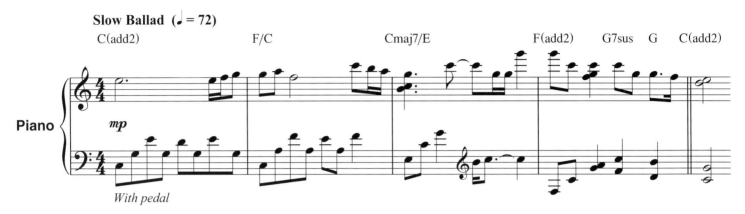

Lady Madonna

Words and Music by John Lennon and Paul McCartney

Just the Way You Are

Words and Music by Billy Joel

Lean on Me

Words and Music by Bill Withers

Let 'Em In

Words and Music by Paul McCartney and Linda McCartney

Let It Be

Words and Music by John Lennon and Paul McCartney

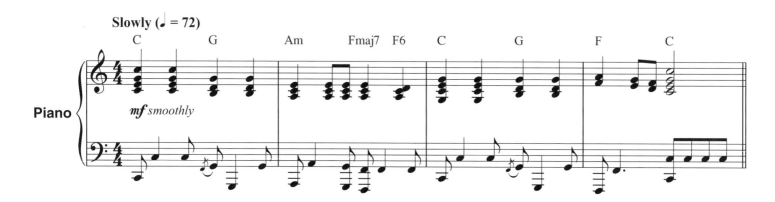

Louie, Louie
Words and Music by Richard Berry

Lovely
Words and Music by Billie Eilish O'Connell,
Finneas O'Connell and Khalid Robinson

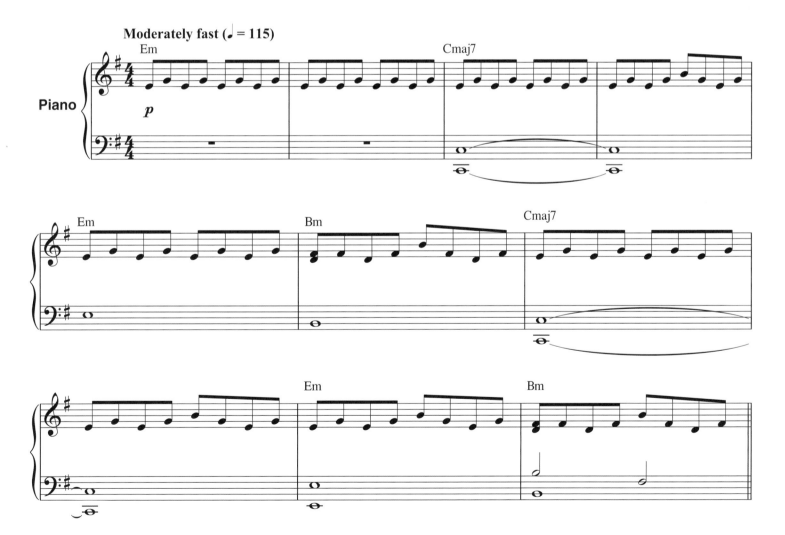

Love Song

Words and Music by Sara Bareilles

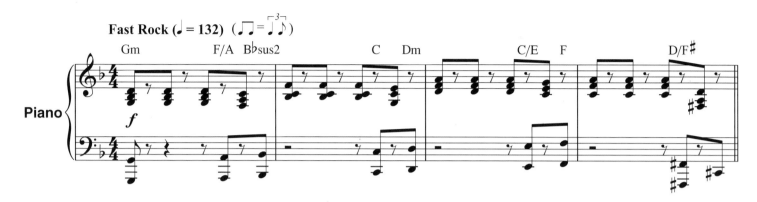

Mandy

Words and Music by Scott English and Richard Kerr

Martha My Dear

Words and Music by John Lennon and Paul McCartney

A Million Dreams
from THE GREATEST SHOWMAN

Words and Music by Benj Pasek and Justin Paul

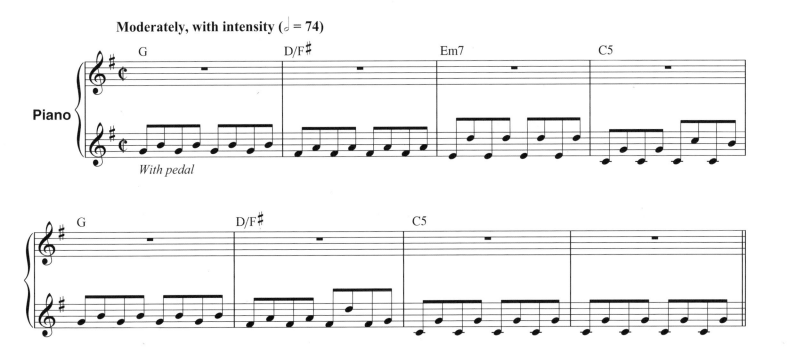

Minute by Minute

Words and Music by Michael McDonald and Lester Abrams

Morning Has Broken

Words by Eleanor Farjeon
Music by Cat Stevens

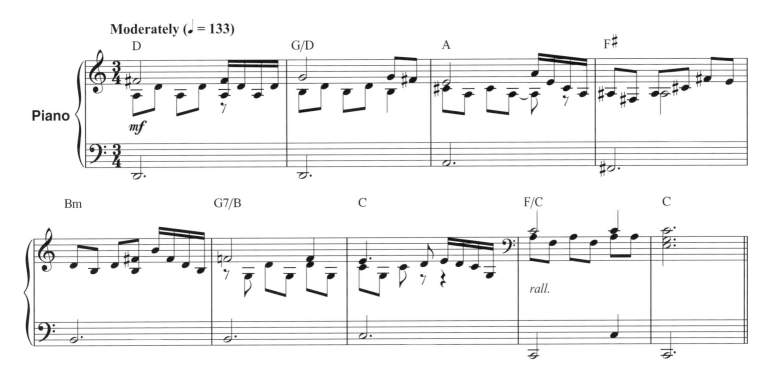

Nobody Does It Better
from THE SPY WHO LOVED ME

Music by Marvin Hamlisch
Lyrics by Carole Bayer Sager

100 Years

Words and Music by John Ondrasik

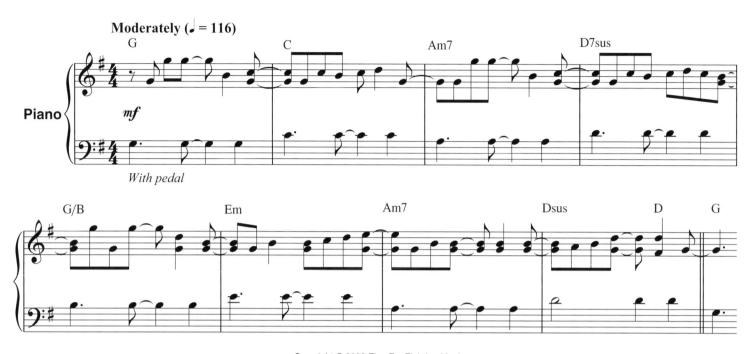

Only the Good Die Young

Words and Music by Billy Joel

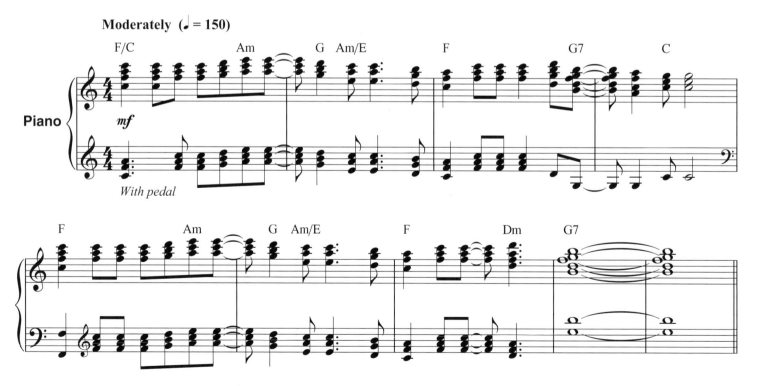

Ribbon in the Sky

Words and Music by Stevie Wonder

Oye Como Va

Words and Music by Tito Puente

Piano Man

Words and Music by Billy Joel

Praying

Words and Music by Kesha Sebert, Ben Abraham,
Ryan Lewis and Andrew Joslyn

Same Old Lang Syne

Words and Music by Dan Fogelberg

Saturday in the Park

Words and Music by Robert Lamm

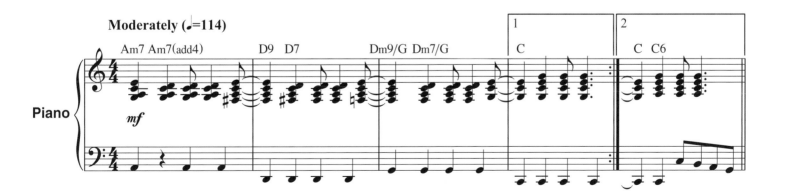

Say Something

Words and Music by Ian Axel, Chad Vaccarino and Mike Campbell

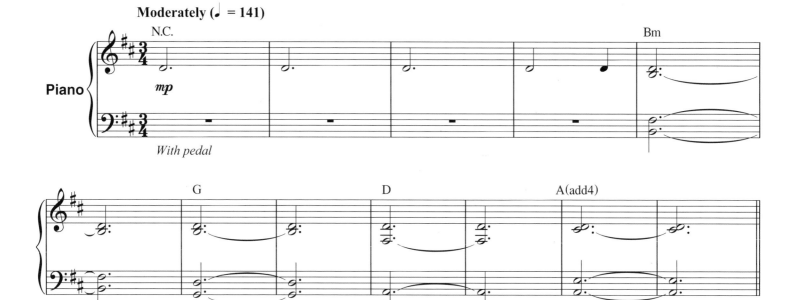

See You Again

from FURIOUS 7

Words and Music by Cameron Thomaz, Charlie Puth, Justin Franks,
Andrew Cedar, Dann Hume, Josh Hardy and Phoebe Cockburn

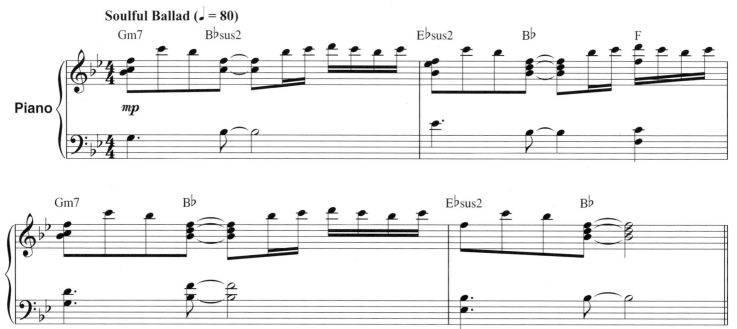

Señorita

Words and Music by Chad Hugo, Pharrell Williams and Justin Timberlake

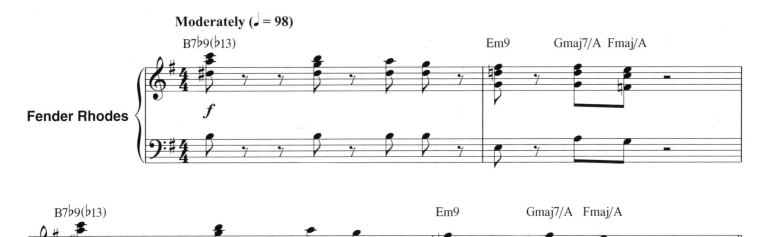

7 Years

*Words and Music by Lukas Forchhammer, Morten Ristorp, Stefan Forrest,
David Labrel, Christopher Brown and Morten Pilegaard*

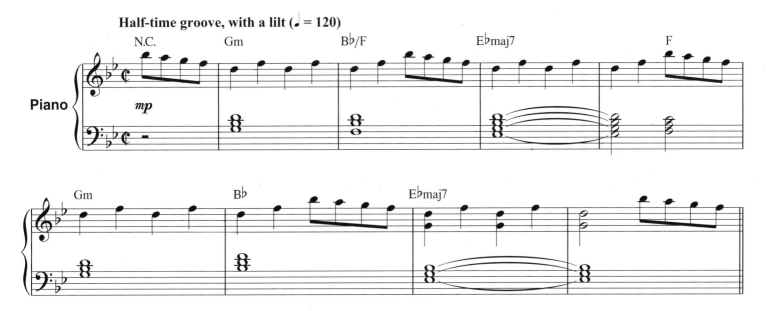

Sister Christian

Words and Music by Kelly Keagy

A Sky Full of Stars

Words and Music by Guy Berryman, Jon Buckland, Will Champion,
Chris Martin and Tim Bergling

Someone Like You

Words and Music by Adele Adkins and Dan Wilson

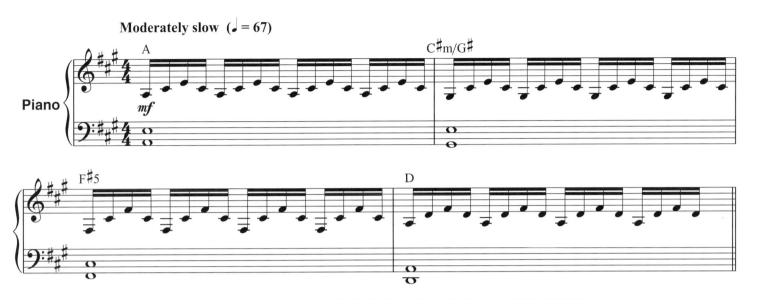

Stay

Words and Music by Mikky Ekko and Justin Parker

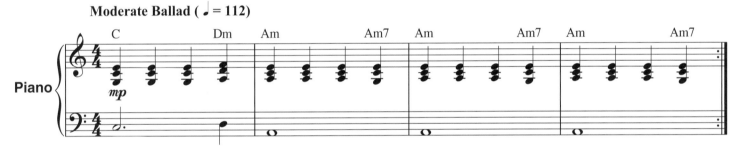

Stay with Me

Words and Music by Sam Smith, James Napier, William Edward Phillips,
Tom Petty and Jeff Lynne

Summer, Highland Falls

Words and Music by Billy Joel

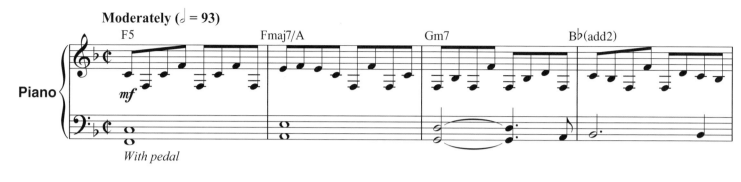

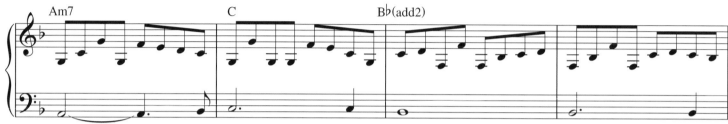

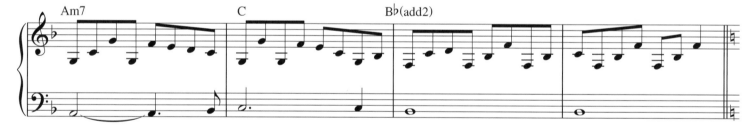

Takin' It to the Streets

Words and Music by Michael McDonald

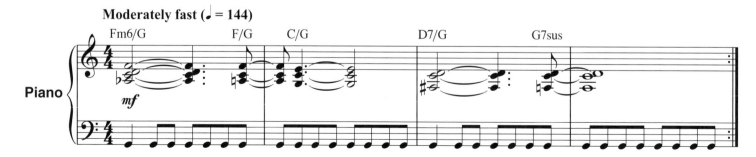

Superstition

Words and Music by Stevie Wonder

Moderately ($\quarternote$ = 104)

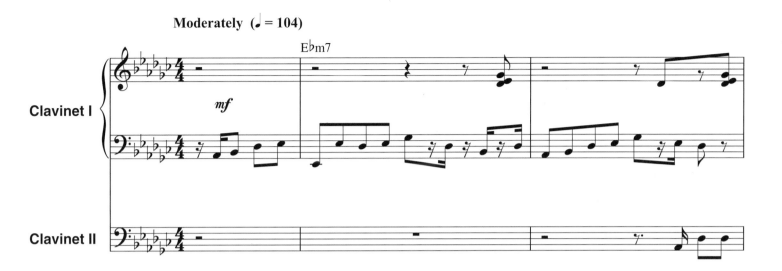

Clavinet I

Clavinet II

Take on Me

Music by Pal Waaktaar and Magne Furuholmne
Words by Pal Waaktaar, Magne Furuholmne and Morton Harket

Still Crazy After All These Years
Words and Music by Paul Simon

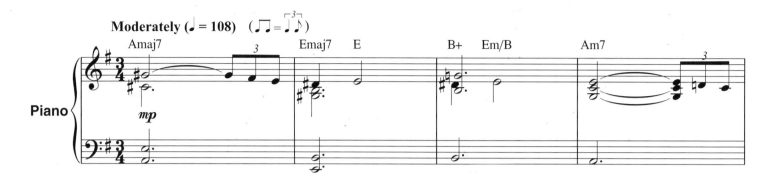

These Eyes
Written by Burton Cummings and Randy Bachman

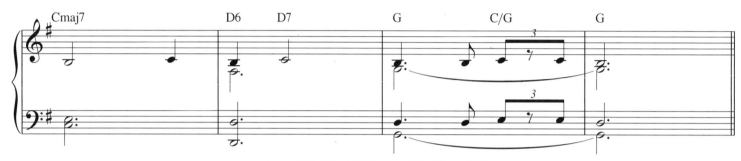

Three Times a Lady
Words and Music by Lionel Richie

This Love

Words and Music by Adam Levine and Jesse Carmichael

A Thousand Miles

Words and Music by Vanessa Carlton

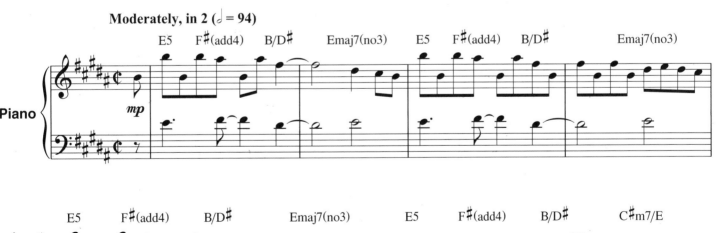

Tiny Dancer

Words and Music by Elton John and Bernie Taupin

Up Where We Belong
from the Paramount Picture AN OFFICER AND A GENTLEMAN

Words by Will Jennings
Music by Buffy Sainte-Marie and Jack Nitzsche

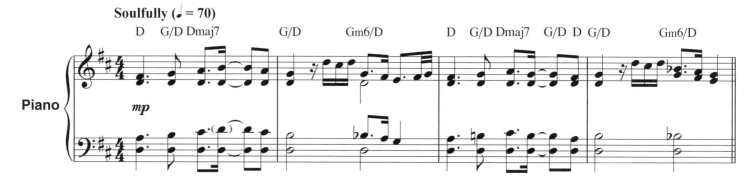

Walking in Memphis

Words and Music by Marc Cohn

The Way It Is

Words and Music by Bruce Hornsby

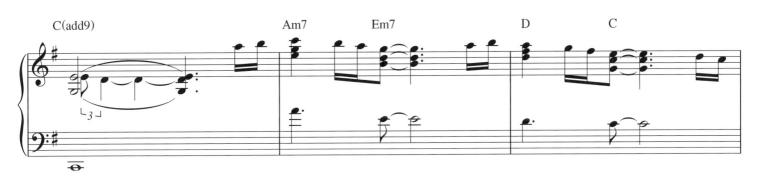

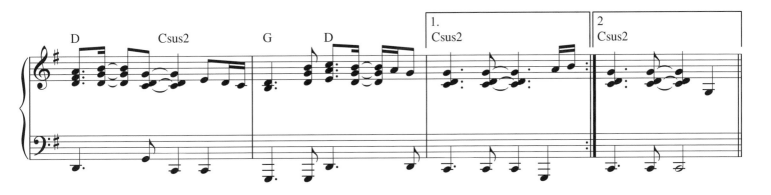

A Whiter Shade of Pale

Words and Music by Keith Reid and Gary Brooker

You Are So Beautiful

Words and Music by Billy Preston and Bruce Fisher

You Are the Reason

Words and Music by Calum Scott, Corey Sanders and Jonathan Maguire

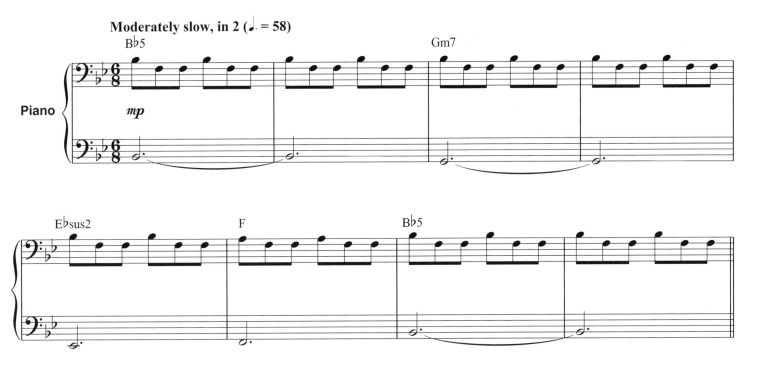

You Are the Sunshine of My Life

Words and Music by Stevie Wonder

You Never Give Me Your Money

Words and Music by John Lennon and Paul McCartney

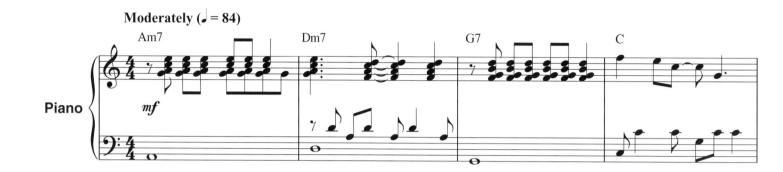

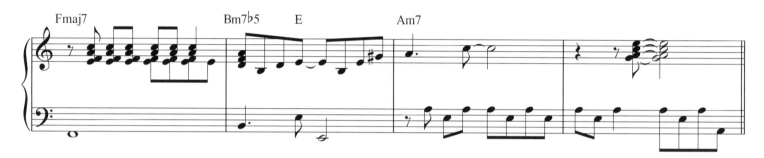

You're My Best Friend

Words and Music by John Deacon

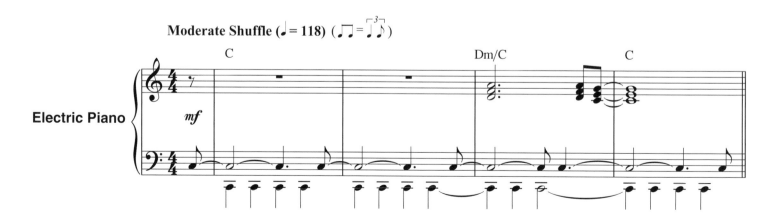

Your Song

Words and Music by Elton John
and Bernie Taupin

Slow, but with a beat (♩ = 63)

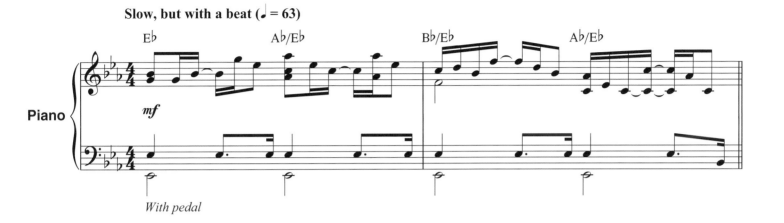

With pedal

Werewolves of London

Words and Music by Warren Zevon,
Robert Wachtel and LeRoy Marinel

Moderate Rock (♩ = 103)

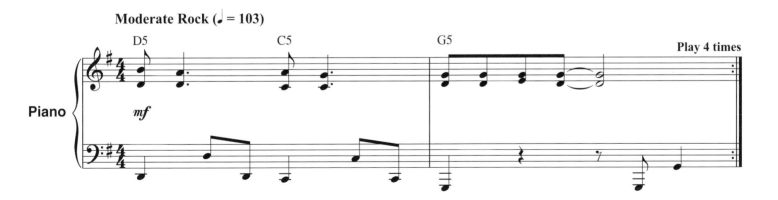

YOUR FAVORITE MUSIC ARRANGED FOR PIANO SOLO

ADELE FOR PIANO SOLO – 2ND EDITION
This collection features 13 Adele favorites beautifully arranged for piano solo, including: Chasing Pavements • Hello • Rolling in the Deep • Set Fire to the Rain • Someone like You • Turning Tables • When We Were Young • and more.
00307585 ....$14.99

PRIDE & PREJUDICE
12 piano pieces from the 2006 Oscar-nominated film, including: Another Dance • Darcy's Letter • Georgiana • Leaving Netherfield • Liz on Top of the World • Meryton Townhall • The Secret Life of Daydreams • Stars and Butterflies • and more.
00313327 ....$17.99

BATTLESTAR GALACTICA
by Bear McCreary
For this special collection, McCreary himself has translated the acclaimed orchestral score into fantastic solo piano arrangements at the intermediate to advanced level. Includes 19 selections in all, and as a bonus, simplified versions of "Roslin and Adama" and "Wander My Friends." Contains a note from McCreary, as well as a biography.
00313530 ....$17.99

GEORGE GERSHWIN – RHAPSODY IN BLUE (ORIGINAL)
Alfred Publishing Co.
George Gershwin's own piano solo arrangement of his classic contemporary masterpiece for piano and orchestra. This masterful measure-for-measure two-hand adaptation of the complete modern concerto for piano and orchestra incorporates all orchestral parts and piano passages into two staves while retaining the clarity, sonority, and brilliance of the original.
00321589 ....$16.99

THE BEST JAZZ PIANO SOLOS EVER
Over 300 pages of beautiful classic jazz piano solos featuring standards in any jazz artist's repertoire. Includes: Afternoon in Paris • Giant Steps • Moonlight in Vermont • Moten Swing • A Night in Tunisia • Night Train • On Green Dolphin Street • Song for My Father • West Coast Blues • Yardbird Suite • and more.
00312079 ....$19.99

ROMANTIC FILM MUSIC
40 piano solo arrangements of beloved songs from the silver screen, including: Anyone at All • Come What May • Glory of Love • I See the Light • I Will Always Love You • Iris • It Had to Be You • Nobody Does It Better • She • Take My Breath Away (Love Theme) • A Thousand Years • Up Where We Belong • When You Love Someone • The Wind Beneath My Wings • and many more.
00122112 ....$17.99

CLASSICS WITH A TOUCH OF JAZZ
Arranged by Lee Evans
27 classical masterpieces arranged in a unique and accessible jazz style. Mr Evans also provides an audio recording of each piece. Titles include: Air from Suite No. 3 (Bach) • Barcarolle "June" (Tchaikovsky) • Pavane (Faure) • Piano Sonata No. 8 "Pathetique" (Beethoven) • Reverie (Debussy) • The Swan (Saint-Saens) • and more.
00151662 Book/Online Audio...$14.99

STAR WARS: THE FORCE AWAKENS
Music from the soundtrack to the seventh installment of the Star Wars® franchise by John Williams is presented in this songbook, complete with artwork from the film throughout the whole book, including eight pages in full color! Titles include: The Scavenger • Rey Meets BB-8 • Rey's Theme • That Girl with the Staff • Finn's Confession • The Starkiller • March of the Resistance • Torn Apart • and more.
00154451 ....$17.99

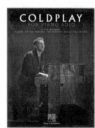

COLDPLAY FOR PIANO SOLO
Stellar solo arrangements of a dozen smash hits from Coldplay: Clocks • Fix You • In My Place • Lost! • Paradise • The Scientist • Speed of Sound • Trouble • Up in Flames • Viva La Vida • What If • Yellow.
00307637 ....$15.99

TAYLOR SWIFT FOR PIANO SOLO – 2ND EDITION
This updated second edition features 15 of Taylor's biggest hits from her self-titled first album all the way through her pop breakthrough album, *1989*. Includes: Back to December • Blank Space • Fifteen • I Knew You Were Trouble • Love Story • Mean • Mine • Picture to Burn • Shake It Off • Teardrops on My Guitar • 22 • We Are Never Ever Getting Back Together • White Horse • Wildest Dreams • You Belong with Me.
00307375 ....$16.99

DISNEY SONGS
12 Disney favorites in beautiful piano solo arrangements, including: Bella Notte (This Is the Night) • Can I Have This Dance • Feed the Birds • He's a Tramp • I'm Late • The Medallion Calls • Once Upon a Dream • A Spoonful of Sugar • That's How You Know • We're All in This Together • You Are the Music in Me • You'll Be in My Heart (Pop Version).
00313527 ....$14.99

UP
Music by Michael Giacchino
Piano solo arrangements of 13 pieces from Pixar's mammoth animated hit: Carl Goes Up • It's Just a House • Kevin Beak'n • Married Life • Memories Can Weigh You Down • The Nickel Tour • Paradise Found • The Small Mailman Returns • The Spirit of Adventure • Stuff We Did • We're in the Club Now • and more, plus a special section of full-color artwork from the film!
00313471 ....$17.99

GREAT THEMES FOR PIANO SOLO
Nearly 30 rich arrangements of popular themes from movies and TV shows, including: Bella's Lullaby • Chariots of Fire • Cinema Paradiso • The Godfather (Love Theme) • Hawaii Five-O Theme • Theme from "Jaws" • Theme from "Jurassic Park" • Linus and Lucy • The Pink Panther • Twilight Zone Main Title • and more.
00312102 ....$14.99

HAL•LEONARD®
7777 W. Bluemound Rd. P.O. Box 13819 Milwaukee, WI 53213
www.halleonard.com